GW01180024

The Hotchpotch Horse

and other stories and poems

Jean Kenward

The Hotchpotch Horse and Other Stories and Poems

Illustrated by
VAL BIRO

Hodder & Stoughton
LONDON SYDNEY AUCKLAND TORONTO

British Library Cataloguing in Publication Data

Kenward, Jean
   The hotchpotch horse and other stories
   and poems.
   I. Title   II. Biro, Val
   823'.914[J]   PZ5

   ISBN 0-340-38971-0

First published 1987

Published by Hodder and Stoughton Children's Books,
a division of Hodder and Stoughton Ltd,
Mill Road, Dunton Green, Sevenoaks, Kent TN13 2YJ

Photoset by Rowland Phototypesetting Ltd,
Bury St Edmunds, Suffolk

Printed in Great Britain by T. J. Press (Padstow) Ltd,
Padstow, Cornwall

Contents

The
Hotchpotch Horse

Once, there was a man who was clever at making things. He was a carpenter, and had neither wife nor children; but he had picked up a stray dog with half a tail, and that was company. Half-a-tail slept under the kitchen table. There was also a cat with half an ear which he had found on a rubbish dump. Half-an-ear slept in the airing cupboard. That was company, too. So there were three of them: Half-a-tail, Half-an-ear, and the carpenter. They were poor, but they almost always had enough to eat. Or nearly enough.

Every morning the carpenter worked in his shed, sawing and hammering: perhaps a book shelf, perhaps a table. Best of all, were the toys. He liked making them; a train, a truck, or a wooden dolly. Sometimes he would sell them. Often, he would give them away. Now and again he would have a big turn-out and make a special thing out of all the bits and pieces that had been left over. But not many customers came.

One day, he was looking through a heap of off-cuts in his shed, when he came upon a broken box.

'Aha! That could be mended,' he said to himself. 'Add four wheels, and you'd have a trolley. Add a handle, and you'd have a push-cart. Add a horse's head, and you'd have –'

'You'd have a hotchpotch!' grunted the dog, and he thumped his half a tail.

The carpenter set to work. It was easy to mend the box, and he put screws in, turning them round and round till they could twist no longer. He cut a lid for the box, that would take right off. He fixed a handle, so that it could be pushed. Then, very carefully, he drew a horse's head on a piece of plywood, and edged round it with his fretsaw.

He stuck the horse's head on firmly with strong, carpenter's glue. He bored a hole for an eye.

'It's a hotchpotch horse, that's what it is,' remarked the cat, washing her half an ear. 'Quite clever, I suppose, but nobody will BUY it.'

'Not bad!' commented the dog, thumping his half a tail. 'Not bad at all. But what's it FOR? Nobody will buy it.'

The carpenter winked. 'How do *you* know?' he questioned. 'It might be useful, one day. *I* like it, anyway. I shall keep it on the front doorstep. Then everybody will see I am a carpenter, and we shall get more custom.'

He varnished the Hotchpotch Horse till its coat shone, although it was only made of bits and pieces, and put it on the front door step with a notice round its neck:

WOODWORK DONE HERE.

People came to look at it. 'Who on earth would want THAT?' they said, and went away again without buying anything at all.

'I told you so!' mewed Half-an-ear. 'We're getting poorer and poorer. One of these days, we shan't have any dinner.'

'What did I tell you?' growled Half-a-tail. 'We're getting thinner and thinner. One of these days we shan't have any tea.'

But the carpenter only winked, and whistled a bit, for he knew better. He knew there was a secret in the heart of things – and who could tell when something might happen?

One morning, something did. He had been working since first light, carving and sanding, smoothing and polishing, sawing and hammering. He had made a set of chess men out of cotton reels. It was really quite grand – there were kings, and queens, and castles. All they needed now was a customer.

The customer who came was not at all the kind they were expecting. She wore a witch's hat, and carried a broomstick under her arm. Half-an-ear was suspicious, and put up her back.

'Bad morning to you!' said the witch, for that was her language. She never used the word 'good' if she could help it. 'I'm looking for a hotchpotch horse to keep my spells in. One with a lid on, you understand, for mischief works best in darkness. I'll give a golden guinea for the one on your front step – it's just what I fancy!'

But the carpenter would not agree. 'I don't sell to witches, and those that make mischief,' he answered. 'Be off, or I'll set the dog on you!'

He lit a candle in the window, and the witch pulled her cloak over her eyes so that she could not see the light, and flew off over the roof tops as smoothly as black treacle.

The Hotchpotch Horse trembled.

'You had better put a heavy stone inside him, so that he can stand firm,' advised Half-a-tail. The carpenter decided that would be a fine idea, and he picked up a large lump of rockery stone and laid it gently inside the Hotchpotch Horse.

No sooner had he returned to his work, than there was a knock on the door.

A wizard stood there, tall as the Post Office Tower.

'Bad morning to you!' whined the wizard, for that was his language. He was always up to something. 'I'm looking for a hotchpotch horse to keep my tricks and serpents in. One with a lid on, you understand, for serpents are best kept in darkness. I'll give you a silver watch chain for the one on your doorstep – it's just what I fancy!'

But the carpenter would not agree. 'I don't sell to wizards, and those that tamper with tricks and serpents. And a watch chain's no use without a watch,' he answered bravely. 'Be off, or I'll set the cat on you!'

He stuck a rose in the window, and the wizard held his nose so that he could not smell it, for he hated perfume, and slid off along the drainpipes as coldly as hoar frost.

The Hotchpotch Horse trembled.

'You'd better put another heavy stone inside him, so that he can stand firm,' advised Half-an-ear. The carpenter decided that was a fine idea, and he picked up a large lump of rockery stone and laid it tenderly inside the Hotchpotch Horse.

There wasn't much for dinner that day, because money had almost run out. In the larder was a rasher of bacon, a crust of bread, and three red cherries.

'What better?' said the carpenter. 'We'll share it between us.'

He divided the food into three. But as they began to eat, the rasher of bacon turned into a hefty York ham, the crust into a new loaf hot from the oven, and the three red cherries into a basket of delicious fruit. There were peaches and pineapples among it, if I am not mistaken.

'You see?' chuckled the carpenter, with a wink.

They ate until they were satisfied, and there was so much left over that they had quite a job to find room in the larder for it all.

That evening, while they were playing chess together with the set made of cotton reels, there was a knock on the door.

'The third today!' marvelled the carpenter. 'But it's late for customers. Maybe someone has lost his way? I'll go and see.'

He opened the door.

Who should be standing there, but the King's messenger himself, with a crown embroidered on his jacket.

'Good evening to you!' he said, rather breathlessly. 'Forgive me for troubling you so late in the day. His Majesty's coach has broken down, and he is urgently in need of a carpenter, for the wheel has buckled. Seeing your notice on the step, the King suggested perhaps you might be able to offer us some assistance? We are stuck fast on the edge of a hill – a *steep* hill, one in four – and are in danger of rolling down!'

'I'll come at once,' answered the carpenter. He seized his bag of tools. 'The wheel buckled? I've a nice bit of wood here that'll put that right. And as to rolling down hill, why, the Hotchpotch Horse will help us.'

He set off, pushing the Hotchpotch Horse

before him, and accompanying the King's messenger. The Hotchpotch Horse had such a weight inside him that the messenger had to push too.

Half-an-ear and Half-a-tail watched them go.

'What's he want the Hotchpotch Horse for?' questioned Half-a-tail, yawning.

'Because of the rockery stones, of course,' snapped Half-an-ear. 'To stop the coach rolling down hill. ANYONE could have thought of THAT.'

'*I* didn't,' answered Half-a-tail, humbly. 'But it's a good idea.'

The King was still sitting in his coach when they reached him, and complained that he had missed his dinner and would miss his supper and his breakfast too if the wheel were not soon mended. The carpenter laid the two heavy stones in front of the back axle, and set to work.

'Why, this is easy!' he said comfortingly as he sawed and hammered. 'It'll be done in a quarter of an hour, or a bit less, I can promise Your Majesty. You'll soon be moving.'

And so it was.

Mending a wheel was easy work to him. When all was finished, the messenger took him to one side.

'The King is anxious to reward you,' he said.

'And he has asked me to enquire whether there is anywhere here he might find something to eat? He would like you to join him.'

'Why, I've eaten my tea but a minute ago,' cried the carpenter, 'but there's plenty over. Tell His Majesty to stop at my cottage, and I'll have it on the table immediately. There's enough for all.'

'Splendid!'

As soon as the wheel was mended, the King was driven to the carpenter's cottage. Six fine stallions drew up at the front door. Was it surprising that food appeared on the table immediately? A York ham, a new loaf hot from the oven, and a basket of delicious fruit. Half-an-ear and Half-a-tail acted as waiters. The carpenter apologised for having no napkins, lit a candle, and winked. When all was over, and the royal coach had departed with much blowing of trumpets and clicking of hooves, the three old friends settled by the fire to talk things over.

'I told you there was a secret in the heart of things,' said the carpenter. The King had presented him with a golden sovereign, and a silver watch chain with a watch to go with it. What is the use of one without the other? He spun the sovereign round, and watched it glinting. He held the watch to his ear, and listened to its tick.

The Hotchpotch Horse was back on the front step by then, of course. Where else? But the notice round his neck had been curiously altered.

Under WOODWORK DONE HERE, it said BY APPOINTMENT TO HIS MAJESTY, in capital letters.

After that, customers came so thick and fast that the carpenter had some difficulty in keeping up with them.

'It's a funny thing,' grunted Half-a-tail, 'but there's always food in the larder, now.'

'Of *course* there is,' mewed Half-an-ear. 'Haven't we had the King to supper? Or tea? Call it what you like. He might come again! You never know. He might want a rasher of bacon. He might want a game of chess. Such things do happen.'

'Such things do happen,' agreed Half-a-tail wisely. 'But most of them are secret.'

The carpenter gave a wink, and a whistle. He didn't actually say anything. After all, what was there else to be said?

Old Mister Pendulum

Old Mister Pendulum,
Tick-tack-tock,
Lives inside
The Gran'pa clock.
I've never seen him
But I know
He's in there;
I hear him go
WHIRR and DING DONG
With his chime
Every day
At dinner-time

Old Mister Pendulum
Talks all night –
Tick-tack-tock
By candlelight –
Tock and tick
When the moon's around,
Spilling silver
On the ground;
Tick and tock
When the sun's up high,
Dropping gold beams
From the sky.

The Hotchpotch Horse

Mister Pendulum's
Calm and cool
Always
When I go to school.
Indoors, it is
Still and quiet . . .
He likes silence
For his diet;
He likes cobwebs,
Dark and dust,
And then he ticks
Because he must.

Tick and tock
And tick-tack-tock.
Mister Pendulum's
In his clock.

The Mischievous
Brass Goblin

A man and a woman once lived together in great contentment, for although they had few possessions they had the gift of happiness – which was lacking in many a rich man's home. The husband was strong and cheerful. He worked for a furniture removal company. It was his job to help people who were moving house, and to carry their tables and chairs and beds and pianos and gas stoves from the old place to the new.

The wife worked in the garden when it was fine. When it was wet, she stayed in the kitchen and made bread. She could sew, too.

One day, the husband was busy helping with a big removal. What a load of furniture there was to pack up! The owners of the house were important people, and it seemed they had something of everything. It was quite a job to get it all into the van. Whew! He stopped for a moment, and wiped the sweat from his face. As he did so, a strange object caught his eye. What was that, among the dust and paper on the floor of the van? Hard and shiny, carved in the shape of a goblin, and with a curious glint to it?

He bent down and picked it up.

It was a brass door knocker.

'That's odd,' said the man to himself. 'People don't usually take their door knockers when they move house. Or, if they do, they wrap them up carefully and tell us. Who can it belong to?'

He made a few enquiries. Nobody knew anything about a brass door knocker.

'I'd better leave it at the police station,' he decided. 'Someone might be looking for it. It might be lost.'

And he went on with his work.

That night, the man got home late, for he had had a long day, with a long journey at the end of it. He had forgotten all about the brass door knocker, until his wife, when she gave him a kiss, felt something hard in his pocket.

'What is it?' she asked.

'It's a door knocker,' said the man. 'I meant to leave it at the police station, but I forgot.'

'I'll take it,' promised his wife. 'I'll run round with it tomorrow morning, after breakfast.' And she put it on the mantelshelf, so that she should remember.

Next morning, after she had said goodbye to her husband, she picked up her duster and started to do her housework. The brass door knocker stood in the middle of the mantelshelf, and glinted. Try as she might, the woman could not take her eyes from it.

'I had better get rid of it at once,' she decided, and put on her mackintosh – for it was raining.

'It's a very UNUSUAL door knocker. There's something disturbing about it.' She gave it a rub.

Immediately, the brass goblin began to talk.

'*Hang me, hang me on your door*
And I will give you wishes four!'

The woman was so surprised that she almost dropped it. Had she been mistaken? Had there really been a voice?

She rubbed the knocker again.

'*Hang me, hang me on your door*
And I will give you wishes four!'

sounded, for the second time.

'How astonishing! Well – there's no harm in trying.' She went to the front door, took down the old knocker (which was falling to pieces), and replaced it with the brass goblin. The rain was coming down harder than ever.

'O dear – look at that, now! I wish I had a decent pair of galoshes!' muttered the woman, without thinking.

Immediately she found herself wearing a huge pair of new galoshes.

'What a bit of luck! I might as well keep the knocker for a bit longer if THIS is what is going to happen,' she cried in excitement. Clump clump, out she went to dig the garden. But alas! When she came in again and tried to remove the

galoshes, she could not. She pulled and she pulled, she tugged and she tugged, this end and that, but nothing would loosen them, big though they were. Soon, there was mud all over the house. The poor woman became more and more distressed. Coming home that evening, her husband was amazed to see her cooking supper with her galoshes on. She did not like to tell him what she had done.

That night she slept with her feet on top of the blankets, to keep mud off the sheets.

In the morning, up and dressed, she again prepared to take the door knocker to the police station. Someone might be looking for it. But she could not resist giving it a rub.

'*Keep me – do not part with me –*
And I will give you wishes three,'

chanted the goblin.

'Again?' marvelled the woman. 'I must be more careful this time. But I do wish I had a scarf on. It's cold here, on the front step, and feels like frost.'

That very moment she found herself wearing a huge woollen scarf – why, I believe it must have been twelve metres long – warm, and cosy.

'What a waste of a wish! Still, at least it's

comfortable,' commented the woman. And out she went to dig the garden. But the moment she stopped, to prepare dinner, she found she was unable to take the scarf off. She pulled and she pulled, in vain. She had to put her apron on top of it.

That evening, when her husband returned, he was taken aback to see her wearing a scarf twelve metres long, as well as galoshes. When bedtime came, she settled down in the armchair, because nobody wants to get into the sheets wearing a scarf and galoshes, too, do they?

'What's come over you, wife?' asked the man in bewilderment.

The woman gave no reply.

She did not like to tell him that she had not yet taken the knocker to the police station.

At last, it was Saturday; a special Saturday, because the couple had been invited to a wedding, and were to put on their best clothes.

'One thing is certain, my dear,' argued the man. 'You cannot go to a wedding wearing a pair of galoshes and a scarf twelve metres long. It would look ridiculous. Everybody would laugh. Let us try once more to pull them off.'

They tried and they tried, but it was useless. Neither the scarf nor the galoshes would budge an inch.

'Well, there it is!' said the man helplessly. 'For my part, I'm going to get ready. You'll just have to stay behind.'

At this, the wife burst into tears, for she enjoyed weddings and had been looking forward to an outing. Why, she had even made herself a new dress, and was eager to wear it.

'I'll try the door knocker once more,' she told herself. 'After all, everything may yet go right. And my husband has not noticed it. Goodness knows what he would wish for, were he to see it!'

She waited until he had gone into the bathroom to shave himself, and then quickly ran to the front door and began to rub the knocker.

'*Wishes two, wishes two*
Remain for me to give to you!'

chanted the goblin.

'I wish – I wish for a wedding hat,' called the woman, clasping her hands. 'A tall one,' she added.

Immediately, she found herself wearing a hat the height of a telegraph pole. It was SO tall that she could not get into her own front door. SO tall, that the crown of it reached the chimney pots, and the starlings roosting there flew away in a fright, squawking.

'For heaven's sake!' shouted her husband, as he saw the hat appearing in front of the bathroom window. He ran downstairs, razor in hand, his chin covered with soap.

His wife tried and tried to get the hat off, but she could not. Even a tin-opener was of no use.

'It's all the fault of the brass door knocker!' she sobbed.

'The brass door knocker? Is it STILL HERE?'

'It's been on the door since Monday,' wept the woman, 'and if you'd had your eyes open, you could have seen it.'

'So it is!' The man gave the door knocker a wipe with his face flannel. 'It may be that goblin is the cause of all the mischief,' he said. 'You never CAN trust a goblin.'

'*Till you take me off the door,*
I will give you one wish more,'

sounded a faint voice. So *very* faint, it was, that nobody heard it.

'I wish everything was as it used to be,' sniffed the woman. 'What's the good of a hat as tall as a telegraph pole? Or a scarf twelve metres long? And nobody wants to wear galoshes ALL the time!'

No sooner had she closed her mouth that the hat, the scarf, and the galoshes disappeared with a puff and a whistle. There she stood, in her ordinary pinafore, and her ordinary slip-slop slippers. There was nothing the least bit EX-TRAordinary about THEM.

That was a relief, I can tell you.

Pleased that his wife was freed from her en-cumbrances, the man took a hammer and a screwdriver and removed the brass knocker from the front door. He handled it gingerly, because you never knew where you were with goblins, and put it in a shoe box and tied the lid on with string.

'We can leave it at the police station on our way to the wedding,' he said firmly.

So things began to brighten.

'We've seen THAT goblin before,' the policeman told them. 'It's always up to mischief. If it isn't this, it's that. I know where it's going this time. On the rubbish dump!'

The man and his wife went off to the wedding in their best clothes, and were happy. Since then, they have bought themselves a new door knocker, a wooden one, in the shape of a wise, wise owl.

They are not expecting to have any trouble with HIM.

As for the brass goblin . . . I passed the rubbish dump myself the other day, and thought – I THOUGHT – I saw something glint. Underneath a washing tub and a broken sewing machine, it was. I was very much tempted to go and pick it up . . . but I didn't. You never know where you are, with goblins.

There let it stay.

Toucan

I saw in the Zoo a great TOUCAN –
A TOUCAN I saw in the zoo.
I could see it as clearly as you can.
I knew it was one, and not two.

I looked at it two, three and four ways –
I said 'Can you give me a clue
Why a singular TOUCAN is always
Pretending it might have been two?'

The TOUCAN replied in a voice that
Came out of the end of his bill:
'You've asked quite a serious question,
And I'll answer it now – yes, I will.

'My parents, they called me a TOUCAN,
(They were thinking of twins, I suppose),
And because I was only a one-egg,
    and lonely,
They gave me this very large nose.'

King Know-all
and the North Star

Once, when the sea came to the edge of the land, and the land had trees on it, and birds flew, there lived a fine and splendid king. His country was known as the Land of Information. It contained so many books that it was quite difficult for people not to fall over them when they went out shopping. Books were piled, shoulder-high, along the sides of the roads, books lined the bus-shelters and the swimming-pool, and every now and then you might come upon a scholar – pen in hand – seated on a stone and scribbling away as hard as he could go. But the king himself was more clever than any of his subjects. It was said that there was nothing he did not know. In his Palace were 365 rooms, one for each day of the year, and each was fitted up as a library with the volumes arranged in alphabetical order. So on a Monday you could find out all you wanted to know about ants, or aspidistras, or aunties, (since these begin with an A); on a Tuesday, about bears, bananas and balloons, on a Wednesday about cats, cotton, and Christopher Columbus . . . and so on, till by the time you came to the end of the year you had learned so much that you had forgotten the beginning of it.

King Know-all (for that was his name) was not only clever; he was also rich. Visitors from other countries would journey to the Land of Information, and would pay large sums of money in return for advice about this or that. They would come, looking anxious, on bicycles, on ships, on horses, or in helicopters. They would await their turns in the Questioning Room at the Palace, pay their money, and return home looking pleased and satisfied. Some of the questions were quite easy: 'How many peas in a pod?' for example; or 'What is the difference between t'other and which?' or 'How long does it take to fly from somewhere to nowhere and back again?' But some were really difficult, and there were times when King Know-all had to put his head in his hands and think really hard before he could give an answer. Or he had to call in his librarians, and order new volumes and encyclopaedias to be brought to him, and study the pages with a magnifying glass and add things up on his fingers and take away the number he had first thought of. But he always knew in the end. Always.

Now it happened one night that a great gale blew up in the Land of Information. Whewwwwww shrieked the wind. It carried the chimney pots off the smaller houses, whipped the tiles from the roofs and blew the smoke like an enormous grey dragon over the sky. My – that was a night to remember! The scholars tied up their books with string and rubber bands so that the pages should not flap, and shut their windows, and put covers on their candles. For twelve hours the storm continued, but by morning its strength had abated, and there was a deep calm. The King's gardeners were out early, tidying up the lawns and flower beds and making a bonfire out of the twigs and leaves and acorns which had blown down during the night. It was hard work, and they were just settling themselves under a tree to eat their elevenses and put red handkerchiefs over their noses for a snooze, when the wheelbarrow boy came up puffing and blowing in a great state of excitement.

'There's something PECULIAR in the fountain,' he blurted, in between gasps. 'It's gold . . . an' it's pointed . . . an' it glitters!'

'A goldfish, silly,' grunted one of the men.

'It ain't a goldfish, It don't swim.'

'A coloured stone?'

'It ain't a coloured stone. It's floatin'!'

'A bit of gold paper?'

'It ain't a bit of gold paper. I poked it wiv me stick. It's *hard*.'

'Cheese, then? You bin throwing cheese into the fountains? You'll cop it, you will! Wait till His Majesty comes out . . .'

'It ain't cheese. It's *peculiar*, I tell yer. Come an' see.'

The gardeners yawned and grunted and scratched their heads, and stretched themselves. They took a last mouthful of bacon sandwich, and a last swig of tea. They followed the wheel-barrow boy over the lawn, through the coppice, to the rose beds. In the centre of the rose beds stood a fountain, spouting great, fluted spires of water into the sky. At its base was a small pool, that had lilies in it, and fish, and frogs' spawn in early summer. But now there was something else there, too. A huge, gold star drifted among the weeds, shining, and crisp, and bright as barley sugar.

'See? Wot did I tell yer?'

The oldest gardener took a look, and nodded. 'You know what that is?' he queried? 'It's the North Star. Must have been blown down in the night.'

'The North STAR?'

He nodded.

'Be a job to get it up in the sky again, that it will. A real job.'

'We could use the window-cleaning ladder?' suggested the wheelbarrow boy. 'I could climb up to the top rung. I could jump . . .'

'And come down with a good wallop you would, too,' scoffed one of the men.

'Well, we could *shoot* it up, p'raps. Fit it into a catapault, like . . .?'

'And 'ave yer eye gashed out when it toppled, I suppose?'

'What we'll do is this,' decided the head gardener. 'We'll take it to King Know-all, and ask 'is advice.' He cleared his throat, importantly.

'What'll we ask 'im?' squeaked the wheelbarrow boy.

'We'll ask 'im wot are 'is explicit instructions

for the putting back in the sky of the North Star. ''E'll look it up in the encyclopaedia, I wouldn't wonder. Under STAR (fallen).'

'Or "North"' put in another.

'Or "Exhibitions and Emergencies"?'

''E'll know. 'E always knows. Come on. Get your fishing net, boy, and we'll hoik it out.'

The wheelbarrow boy ran off at great speed and came back with his net.

It was quite difficult, catching the North Star. First, it squirmed under the water lily leaves, and they couldn't see it. Then it came up again on the other side of the pool, but so tangled with weeds that the wheelbarrow boy fell in in his excitement and had to be dragged out again and dried before they could continue. At last they managed to shove the net underneath the star, and drew it slowly, very slowly to the edge of the water.

It was extremely beautiful. Its light was so brilliant that they had to cover their eyes at first, and only peep at it between their fingers. Two of its points were caught in the netting, and as the head gardener disentangled it he told the others it felt as hot as fire, yet at the same time, as cold as ice. When it was free they wiped it carefully on their cleaning rags, and wrapped it in a jacket, and laid it in the wheelbarrow on a bed of leaves so that it should not crack or break into fragments when they pushed it. Then they wheeled the barrow very, very delicately to the front door of the Palace, and rang the casualty bell for King Know-all. It was a special bell, only used on urgent occasions, and the King rushed downstairs without stopping to put his slippers on, or even to take the curlers out of his beard. He had been having breakfast in bed, you see, and hadn't expected callers before noon.

'What's this? What's this?' questioned King Know-all sharply. 'I hope it's IMPORTANT. More important than my toast and marmalade. Be quick, please. My cornflakes will be getting soggy.'

'Your Majesty . . . we 'ave 'ere, the NORTH STAR!' stuttered the head gardener. 'And wot we wants to know, Your Majesty, is this: 'ow can we get it up again before nightfall? If we *don't* get it up, the fishermen will lose their way. Why, they may never get 'ome again! Add to that, we shan't 'ave no sardines nor no sprats, no cod, nor kipper, nor 'alibut . . . nor . . .'

' . . . never get 'ome again!' echoed the other gardeners. 'No 'addock, nor 'ake, no plaice, dab, nor lemon sole whatever . . .!'

The wheelbarrow boy was so distressed that he burst into sobs and had to wipe his nose on his shirt tail.

'Put back the North Star?' snapped King Know-all. 'That should be quite simple. One moment, please.' He drew a dictionary out of his pyjama pocket, and looked up 'north'.

'Opposite to south' it said.

Then he looked up 'star'. There was a great deal about stars. The dictionary told him to look in *another* dictionary; and that one told him to

look in yet *another*, and so it went on until they were entirely surrounded with books and encyclopaedias, and the wheelbarrow boy had gone to sleep and was snoring on the page between 'pigsty' and 'pigsticking'.

But there was nothing in any of the books to explain how the North Star could be put back in the sky.

Nothing at all.

The King sent for the finest scholars in the land; then for the schoolmasters and schoolmistresses, and the people who taught in universities and colleges and kitchens and places of learning all over the country. They knew so much that they all talked at once, explaining how This was not always That, but only Sometimes . . . but not one of them knew what to do with a fallen star.

Soon, it began to grow dusk. The King was in despair. 'Can *none* of you help me to find the answer?' he entreated. 'Can *none* of you save the fishermen on the dark sea? Not to mention our delicious sprats and sardines and halibut and sole and haddock and turbot and parsley sauce?'

The scholars shuffled and snorted, and looked embarrassed. But they could not help.

Then night came, and with it the brown owl who lives in the woods.

'Oooo hoo!' he chuckled, when he saw all the people gathered outside the Palace. 'What a to-doooo! What's the matter with youoooooo?'

They told him.

'Why,' hooted the brown owl, 'that's EASY! Just ask the wind to blow the star UP again, that's all! Haven't you thought of that? I know where the wind lives. He's an old friend of mine. I'll ask him myself. Hold on –'

Owl drifted off on his great wings, and the King and the scholars and the gardeners and the wheelbarrow boy sat on the palace steps and waited. A few faint, frail, tiny stars began to appear among wisps of cloud; but where the North Star should have been was a dark patch as thick as india rubber.

Owl was soon back again.

'Wind was asleep,' he explained, 'but I woke him up. I tweaked his overcoat, and he began to bluster immediately. He sends a message to say that he's very sorry about the accident – he never meant to blow the star down at all, but it got tangled up in his shoe buckles and he had to give a kick to get it OFF. Then, it started to fall – and he hadn't time to wait and catch it. Says he'll blow it back up again in half a second. You are to rest it in the top of the aspen tree, and he'll be by in a quarter of an hour.'

The wheelbarrow boy was extremely excited at this, and volunteered to carry the star into the aspen tree himself. 'For I can climb 'igher than the others, sir,' he explained, 'an' I can stuff the star underneath me shirt, between me vest and braces, so's I shan't drop it.'

The King graciously assented. 'Yes, my lad, of course. Carry on immediately. You have my royal permission.'

And the wheelbarrow boy picked up the North Star very gingerly. It was as hot as fire, and as cold as ice. He only opened his eyes a little bit, and looked through the lashes, for he did not want to be blinded. He pushed it in between his shirt and his braces, and with both hands free began to climb the aspen tree . . . up . . . up . . . up. It was easy to climb, and he had just got to the top when the leaves began to rustle and nudge each other. Aspen leaves are sensitive, and can hear things a long way off.

'Be quick!' called the King, hearing the leaves. 'The wind is coming!'

WWWwwwwwwwwwwooossssh!

Just as the wheelbarrow boy balanced the North Star among the branches, the wind tore round the Palace wall and whipped it up into the air. Higher and higher and higher still it blew, twinkling and turning, twirling and twinkling, like a golden butterfly, until it took its proper place among the others, and stayed there, firm and steady, following its proper course over the night . . . guiding those who were lost to their journey's end.

'GOOD!' sighed everybody. 'THAT'S better. NOW the fishermen will be able to find their way home again, and we shall have sardines and sprats for breakfast. And halibut and pilchards and cod and mackerel, and shrimps on toast, maybe, if we are lucky.'

The King was so delighted that he issued a proclamation.

'In future, OWL is to be known as the Wisest in the Land.' He pinned a medal on Owl's breast. 'For there is some information,' he decided, 'which cannot be found in books, and which even the cleverest people in my country do not know!'

'Too-whit!' cried Brown Owl. 'To-what? To-whooooooooo!'

What Do You Say?

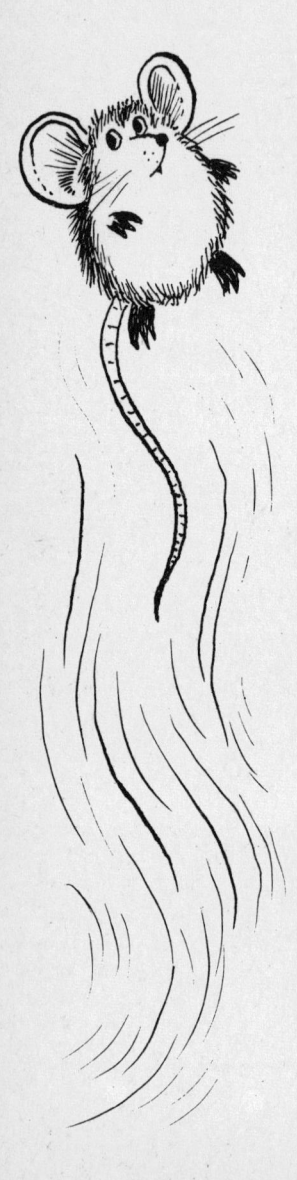

What do you say?
What do you say?
A wind is blowing
A mouse away!

I saw him flying
O – ever so high –
With his tail and whiskers
Over the sky.

I saw him blowing
O – ever so light –
Like a bit of a star
On a winter's night.

I saw him skittering
Over the air . . .
Did YOU ever notice
A mouse up there?

What do you say?
What do you say?
A wind is blowing
A mouse away?

A
Trap for Wizards

Once there was a man who kept a pet shop. You could tell it was a pet shop, even if you had your eyes shut, because of the rich smell of corn and oats and parrot seed and dog biscuits; sacks full of this, and sacks full of that, were piled against the wall. On the other side were the animals and birds waiting to be sold – Dutch rabbits, guinea-pigs, a hamster with her babies, some white mice, and a gerbil or two. They were beautifully kept. The man was proud of his pets, and would only let them go to homes where they were sure to be kindly treated. Sometimes, he had puppies, or a stray kitten that nobody wanted. And occasionally, there was a canary, or a budgerigar.

Every morning, the man whistled as he cleaned out the cages. At five o'clock he made sure that the animals and birds were safe and comfortable before he locked up for the night.

One evening, just as he was giving a last look round before turning the key, he noticed something strange – something, you might say, a bit peculiar. The canary, who usually sang so prettily, wasn't singing any more.

'What's the trouble?' asked the man, tapping the cage with his finger.

The canary sat with his head under his wing, and didn't answer.

'Lost your voice, have you? Lost your whistle, eh?'

He opened the cage door, and let the canary out. It was used to coming out, and would often fly round the shop, perching here and there, and giving a vibrant trill of song as it did so. But that evening, it didn't.

It just sat still, opening and closing its beak. And not a sound was heard.

What in the world was wrong?

'I can tell you,' squeaked one of the hamsters. 'A wizard came in. He came in when you weren't here. Stole the canary's voice, he did, and popped it into a tin he was carrying. He was out again before you could say cat's whiskers.'

'STOLE his voice?'

'That's common practice, among wizards. They keep a collection of voices. Useful, you know . . .'

'Useful?'

Here, a guinea-pig joined in.

'Of course they're useful. *For pretending to be somebody else*, you understand. We guinea-pigs lost our tails to wizards, long ago. A spare fur coat . . . a spare tail . . . a spare set of toe nails . . . a spare voice . . . and hey presto! You're different!'

'I don't know about that,' mused the shop-keeper. 'But one thing's certain. We must get the canary's voice back. No one will give a home to him without a voice. We must FIND it. And as soon as possible, too. But how?'

He put the bird carefully back into its cage, locked up, and went to bed.

That night, he could not sleep. He tossed and turned, threw off the covers and pulled them on again, got up for a drink of water, tried thinking of Christmas. It was no good. A few minutes before morning he dropped into a light doze – and immediately the alarm clock woke him with a clatter.

At the sudden noise, an idea flew into his head.

'I know!' said the shopkeeper to himself. 'The thief MIGHT come into the shop again. He might come in disguise, in search of other voices; a mew, or a growl, for instance. A squeak, or a squawk. I must make a trap.'

A TRAP for wizards.

There must be an instruction book, SOME-WHERE.

After breakfast, he worked in the pet shop as usual. He stared very closely at each customer, every time there was a clang of the bell, but nobody came in who looked in the least like a wizard. At dinner-time, he went to the library, and looked up 'Wizards: how to discover and trap them' in the encyclopaedia.

Not much was helpful. 'Wizards,' it said, 'have remarkable powers. Can be kindly, but are sometimes dangerous. Treat with care. Difficult to trap. Try pepper.'

And that was all.

The shopkeeper closed the encyclopaedia, wrote PEPPER on the back of an envelope, and returned to the shop. And while he was giving the animals a clean out, he noticed other things. A box of cat bells was missing. That was odd, because it had only arrived yesterday, and was just opened. And a dog basket, one of the expensive kind with a cushion to go with it, had completely disappeared.

'Bother!' said the man. 'This won't do. We can't have people helping themselves, wizards or no. I'm not leaving the place until I catch him!'

And he kept his word. The man rang up the

baker and asked him to send sandwiches round, as he wouldn't be going home to eat. Later, he rang again and asked for sausage rolls. 'And send a pot full of pepper with them,' he added. And at closing time, when he had settled all the animals and birds for the night, he rolled himself in a stripy horse blanket and lay down behind the counter with a sack of chicken meal for a pillow.

For some time, nothing happened. It grew darker, of course. The outside noises of cars and buses and bicycle bells died away, and instead he could hear a couple of owls calling to each other . . . and even a bat, piping. The clock on the church tower struck nine, ten, eleven – and then, at last, twelve.

Now, everybody knows that twelve o'clock at night is a witching hour. Why, absolutely ANY- THING might happen. So the shopkeeper kept his eyes wide, wide open, and dared not shut them even for a second. And on the exact stroke of twelve, there was a most extraordinary sound. It was a mixture of a rustle and a swoop. The key of the door fell to the ground with a shrill clatter, and in came – well, I don't know WHAT you would call him. For one thing, although he had the face of an old, old man, he appeared to be as spry and nimble as a young one; he wore red stockings (which you would not have expected),

and a ring of bells round each of them at knee
level. 'CAT bells?' the shopkeeper asked himself, in a whisper. The visitor carried an ancient
tin box under his arm, with a notice on it:
WORDS and VOICES, TAILS and NOISES.
He glanced round the shop with his bright,
bright eyes, which shone as if there were a star in

each of them. Then he began to move toward the cage with five tortoiseshell kittens in it, leaping, and dancing as he went, so that the bells rang and jingled. As he moved, he sang something that sounded like this:

'I'm a collector of voices –
Yes, I'm a collector of sound.
I'm after all manner of noises,
I keep both my ears to the ground!
I look for a growl or a whistle,
I look for a grunt or a squawk –
I steal all the words that are lying around
When the parrot is learning to talk!
I'm a collector of voices.
If you happen to have one today
Be sure, I shall certainly find it
And lock it securely away – aha!
And lock it securely –
ATISHOO!'

The shopkeeper leaned over the counter, holding the stripy horse blanket round him with one hand, and shaking the pepper pot violently with the other.

'ATISHOO ATISHOO ATISHOO! Stop! Stop! Put it away!' gasped the Wizard. 'I can't BEAR pepper. It puts me out! It makes me ordinary! It spoils my magic! Atishoo!'

'And a good thing too!' the shopkeeper told him, flourishing the pepper pot in his hand and teasing the last few grains out of it. 'What do you think you are up to? Those are MY cat bells. Give them back this minute. And where's the dog basket? What about my canary? That was a PRIZE voice, that was – he NEEDS it. He needs it NOW.'

'Atishoo! Atishoo! Half a minute!' squeaked the wizard. He tore off the cat bells and tossed them on to the counter. Then he opened his tin . . . crrrrk! It was a bit rusty, (with age, I suppose), and there was a picture of stars and moons on the lid, gold and silver. Inside were a great number of tiny packets, each one about the size of a postage stamp and wrapped in smooth, shiny paper that glittered – blue, yellow, pink, green, orange, red, purple – every colour you could think of and even some you had never seen before.

'Put the pepper pot away!' begged the wizard, rubbing his eyes. 'The canary's voice is wrapped in yellow. Yellow's for high voices, red's for angry ones, purple's for low ones, and so on. HERE is it!'

He took out a tiny, pale yellow packet, a sort of mimosa colour, and shook it gently.

Immediately, the canary began to sing.

'*I* can't see a voice,' protested the shopkeeper, doubtfully.

'Of course you can't. No one can SEE voices, except me. And it's not really a case of seeing . . . it's a case of *recognising*. It's a case of Being Aware Of. Understand?'

The shopkeeper didn't entirely understand, but he did nearly.

'I'm keeping pepper in this shop *always*,' he warned. 'From now on, there'll be a fresh pot on the counter every day, newly filled. You ought to be ASHAMED of yourself. Wizards are supposed to do GOOD things, not bad ones, with their magic. And what about my dog basket?'

'It's in the moon,' muttered the wizard. 'I live there. It's cold, I can tell you, when there are no clouds around to wrap oneself up in, and the moon is full. I've always fancied a basket to sleep in – always. With a cushion. I can bring it back.' He shivered a little, and a tear ran down his nose. He must have been feeling cold even then, because it made a faint tinkle as if it had been turned to ice. You could tell it wasn't a warm, human tear at all. And the shopkeeper began to feel a little sorry for him. At last, 'You can keep the dog basket,' he decided 'but only if you work for it.'

'WORK for it?'

'On Saturday nights. Clean the shop out for me every Saturday, after closing time. It's always dirty on Saturdays, because we get a lot of customers. YOU clean it, and then I can go along to the Bingo Hall and enjoy myself.'

So the wizard agreed to clean the shop on Saturday nights, in return for the dog basket. And he kept his word.

There wasn't any more trouble about stealing things. You may be sure of that. The shopkeeper left a pepper pot on the counter as a warning, and one of those little twisting mills beside it, so that the pepper would always be fresh. As for the canary – I think the wizard must have bewitched him a little, (or perhaps it was something to do with the shiny papers), for after the voice had been returned to him he sang much more loudly . . . more loudly than ever before . . . and in a different sort of way. Indeed, some of the customers believed him to be a nightingale, and wrote to tell the Queen.

I have been told she is extremely busy spring cleaning, but she is coming to hear him as soon as she has a spare half day.

Goodness!

All Sizes and Shapes

All sizes and shapes
Are the elves and the fairies.
You can't tell what colour
Their skin or their hair is:
You don't know the size
Of their ears or their noses,
Nor whether their hats
Are as small as egg cosies.

The Hotchpotch Horse

All mixtures and moulds
Are the gnomes and the ogres,
The giants and genies
And goblins and bogies;
But never a shadow
They let fall behind them,
And never a footprint
To tell where to find them.

All darkness and daubs
Are the wizards and witches!
They skip over mountains
And scuttle in ditches.
You hear them about
But you're never quite certain –
O, listen! What's that?
Only wind in the curtain . . .

The Man
Who Loved Peacocks

Once there was a man who loved peacocks. You might think that a rather peculiar way to begin a story; but after all, one has to begin somewhere, and it IS rather a peculiar story.

He lived in a curiously-shaped cottage on the edge of a river that had turned itself into a lake and back again. The cottage had three corners, and a low window in each one of them. Out of the windows you could see a field with two donkeys in it, some wood pigeons, and maybe a dog with a long, tatty coat, mooching around and looking for things. The donkeys were old – very old. You could guess that, because their eyes were tired, and the skin on their backs worn thin. They had been working donkeys for many years down in the city, when the man had found them, and brought them home. He had bargained for them, and a whole week's money had gone toward their purchase. Sim and Sam, he called them. They were resting. The dog had been a stray – make no mistake about that. Why, where on earth had he come from? Nobody knew. He loved his master dearly, and the titbits he had for dinner and tea every day – but he wasn't much good as a watch dog. He was friendly, you see, and rather shy. He only barked on Sundays, when the church bells were ringing. I expect he believed he was joining in.

The man had valuables in his curiously shaped cottage: jewellery. He was himself a jeweller, and was thought by some to be the finest in the world. But he was ugly to look at, being extremely small, and with a hump on his shoulder which had grown as a result of an accident that he had suffered when he had been a baby. He limped, too, for one leg was a little shorter than the other. But the people who visited him to admire his jewellery, and to order some for important occasions, did not notice how odd was his appearance. They were caught, instantly, by his eyes which were of a brilliant blue; and, of course, by the intense beauty of the jewels themselves. Rings, bracelets, lockets, necklaces – even coronets. Some were of gold, and some of silver. Many were studded with precious stones – and there were a few which were wonderfully contrived out of pure amber, onyx, rock crystals, opal, and topaz.

The jeweller kept his goods on flat trays, just inside the windows, so that people who were passing on foot – or perhaps having a river picnic – might look at them. By this means, he earned a fairly reliable living; not much, for it took a long time to make a necklace, but enough. It was his ambition to set up a home for animals that had been unkindly treated. The donkeys, and the dog, were a beginning. After them, came the peacocks.

The jeweller had always loved peacocks. He visited a local botanical garden frequently, to admire the splendid birds which marched to and fro on the terrace, opening their great tails, and showing a thousand multi-coloured eyes and calling to each other. When he heard that they proved too damaging to the flowers, and were to be destroyed, he was very upset. He had rather a wild garden, himself; cow parsley, primroses, bluebells and foxgloves grew in it profusely; and at the brink of the water there were kingcups, too, among the rushes. He liked it that way, and offered a price for the peacocks. He did not think that they would do any harm.

'Not enough! Not enough!' commented their keeper. 'Not enough at all. If you want royal birds, you must pay royal money.' He intended to kill them, you see, and sell their feathers to decorate the hats for the aristocracy.

So the jeweller saved up MORE money. He sold a silver coronet, crusted with tiny pearls, to a visiting princess. She gave him gold coins for it, and he took the money immediately to the keeper. He was only just in time, for the man was sharpening his knife.

The birds were too big to carry, so he put them very carefully, one after the other, on his wheel-barrow, and trundled them home, lip-lop, lip-lop, all the way. They soon settled at their new address, and were often to be heard giving a piercing shriek, which quite frightened people until they realised what it was.

'It's their conversation,' explained the jewel-ler. 'Or, their song, as you might say. You may feel it is unpleasant – but only look how beauti-ful they are when they spread their tails! After all, not one of us is perfect . . .'

The visitors agreed that it WAS a beautiful sight, and they brought out their cameras and took photographs.

And now the jeweller found he had to spend a lot of money on feeding his animals. Winter was coming on. The donkeys needed a stable, and some warm hay. They liked a dish of hot bran mash occasionally, too, for they felt the cold severely. The jeweller cut them a jacket each, out of an old hearth rug, with two holes for their front legs so that it would not blow away. The stray dog slept in a box under the kitchen table, so HE was all right; and for the peacocks he put up a wooden shelter, proofed against rain and snow, and with windows to let in the light. It was quite close to the wall of his cottage, and the peacocks took a great interest in the arrival of

new customers. They liked to show themselves off. Sometimes, a loose feather drifted from their beautiful tails. When this happened, the jeweller would take it indoors and study the pattern and the colours closely, through a magnifying glass.

Then he would work away with his tools and copy the feather, in the shape of a brooch, using amber, onyx, rock crystals, opal and topaz.

One day, he completed what he believed to be the finest brooch he had ever made. It was the exact shape of a peacock's feather, and he had used an amethyst for the centre of each circle in the pattern. How it shone! And how it curved, too; not too much, but gently, like a young and slender moon. The jeweller stood back to admire it, and clasped his hands. At such times, he would forget his own, ugly body. He seemed to live in the beauty of what he had designed, and gradually it absorbed his whole self.

Many people came to look at the feather brooch, but it was expensive. It lay in the centre of a window, poised on a piece of dark velvet. The jeweller began to think he would never sell it. Then, suddenly, a customer appeared with small, black eyes, long, curly hair, and a hat like a round pill-box on his head. He had come from the other side of the world to look at the feather brooch, for he was a merchant, and was keen to add to his stock. His eyes glittered, as he pressed his nose to the window. At last, he entered the cottage, and began to bargain. The jeweller was pleased to receive a customer, but soon discovered that the merchant was fooling him.

'They are not precious stones!' scoffed the man. 'Anyone can see they are artificial. Made of bottle-glass, I dare say, and the workmanship is coarse. I can only offer very little for such an object.'

'Alas!' answered the jeweller, 'I could not feed my animals on such a small sum. The stones are real, and are worth a great deal more. Why, there is a giant opal among them. Can you not see it?'

'Rubbish!' snapped the foreigner. He turned his back on the jeweller, and slammed the door.

That night, the dark stranger could not sleep, but tossed and turned in his bed until morning. Then, just as the sun was rising, he had an idea.

'Of course!' he chuckled. 'That's it! I'll STEAL the brooch. What better? The dog's a softie and won't bark if I stroke its head and talk to it gently . . . it'll be an easy job. Easy. I'll nick it this evening, when darkness is falling and the jeweller's having his tea.' Having come to a decision, he turned on his side and fell fast asleep, snoring heavily, until noon.

It so happened that there was a fog around that

evening, and a frost too. At tea time, the jeweller shut up shop and resigned himself to the fact that there wouldn't be any more customers that day. He was anxious. Money was scarce. There were more bills to pay in the winter, and the summer trippers had packed up until better weather should come.

'No matter!' he comforted himself. 'We'll manage, somehow.' He opened a tin of baked beans, and shared it equally on two plates; one for himself, and one for the dog.

When they had eaten, the dog retreated to his box under the kitchen table, for a snooze. The jeweller got out his account books, and began to add up. He wasn't much good at arithmetic; he used a wooden frame, with beads on it arranged in tens to make it easier. Then, drawing a neat line under his total, he went to bed. It was a very SMALL total, and the sooner it was put out of mind the better.

It was while the jeweller was tucking the blankets round himself, and making sure his one good foot didn't stick out the end, that he heard the peacocks.

'Why aren't they in their shed?' he pondered. But they weren't. Again and again came that harsh, high-pitched shriek. And underneath it – wasn't that the sound of breaking glass?

The jeweller crept out of bed, pulled on his dressing-gown, and stumped downstairs.

The window pane was broken. There were fragments of glass all over the place – it was a good job he had absent-mindedly pushed his toes into his slippers, or he might have cut himself. Worst of all – the jewelled feather had gone!

But not for ever. Here comes the surprise in my story. You remember Sim and Sam, the two old donkeys? THEY heard something unusual going on, and being inquisitive (like most donkeys) made their way through the fog to find out what it might be. There, in the peacocks' shed, with the great birds guarding the door, their glorious tails magnificently extended, crouched a man with black eyes, long, curly hair, and a sort of pill-box on his head. But what was he clutching in his hand? Something that shone and glittered like a waterfall of stars. It was the jewelled feather.

Sam and Sim immediately began to add their own noise to that of the peacocks. EE AW! HEE HAW! Like that, but more so. Having no telephone, the jeweller could not ring for the police, but he ran up the road on his gammy leg, plip-plop, and tugged the rope that hung from the church bell. No sooner did the bells begin to peal, than the dog began to bark. HE thought it was Sunday, I suppose. And before you could count up to ten – even with a frame to help you – the local policeman had arrived, wearing a tall helmet with a nob on top of it, and the thief was captured.

He had to give back the jewelled feather, of course, and a big fine to go with it. More than a hundred pounds! It would be enough to feed the jeweller and his family for weeks. So many people had heard the peacocks and the donkeys and the dog and the church bells all going at once that they made a point of visiting the jeweller and inspecting his new window as soon as possible. From that time forth, he began to sell – not just once a month, or once a week, but every day.

Quite soon, he had enough money for the purchase of another donkey . . . then another . . . then another . . . till there were twenty-five of them altogether. Twenty-five donkeys take a long time to feed, so the jeweller advertised for assistance. He gave the job to a man with black eyes, and long curly hair, with a hat like a pill-box on his head.

'You see, I was sorry for him,' he explained. 'And he's extremely good with animals. Dog enjoys his company.'

The peacocks, he always looked after himself.

After all, it was they who were responsible for the comfortable state of affairs. It was lucky for *him* they had made such a noise when they did, with their crude and raucous voices, wasn't it? And he had always loved peacocks, anyway.

As for the jewelled feather: it was bought by the mayor of that town for a very large sum of money indeed. He wears it only on the most important occasions.

One day, perhaps, you may see it.

Chalk Lion

I saw a lion
On Whipsnade Hill:
His face was round
As a daffodil,

And out of chalk
His one green eye
Stared at the weather
And the sky –

Stared and stared
As if to say,
'Not many lions
Walk this way.'

Chalk Lion

Sometimes, when it snows,
I guess
That he wears whiteness
Like a fleece,

Whiteness covers
Cheek and nose,
Smothers whiskers,
Tail and toes,

And whiteness
Rubs him out, until
There is no lion
On Whipsnade Hill.

The
Golden Needle

Once, many years ago, there lived a small man with a crooked back and no hair. He was a tailor. All day he sat in his little room, close to the window (for his eyes were not very good), sewing . . . sewing . . . sewing. His work was extremely fine, for he made suits for the highest people in the land, and they wanted the seams to be wholly invisible and the stitches as dainty as caraway seeds.

One day, when he had been working since early morning, and had taken only a piece of bread for his dinner, a starling came close to the window.

'Squeak,' whistled the starling – for that was his kind of conversation, 'I have caught my leg on some barbed wire. Can you mend it for me, with button thread?'

The tailor stopped his sewing, and opened the

window so that the starling could step inside.

'Dear me! That's a nasty thing!' he muttered, looking closely at the wound. 'A bit of button thread, yes, and perhaps a matchstick splint. How's that?'

'Much better! Much better!' shrilled the starling, and he flew off bravely, taking a beakful of crumbs with him as a present for his wife.

The tailor sighed, and stretched himself.

'Whew! Whew!' whispered a butterfly, (for that was her kind of language). She had been sleeping behind the curtain, and her wings were painfully stiff. 'How I long for the sun! But some of my colours need dusting; they appear quite faded after the winter. Have you time to spare, for I think you could help me?'

'Time belongs to no man,' answered the tailor. 'You can certainly share some of mine.' He gently puffed the dust off her wings with a tiny pair of bellows.

'How's that?'

'Muchchch betterrrr!' whispered the butterfly. She unfolded her wings as wide as they would go, and quivered with joy. The tailor lifted her carefully and put her on a green plant that stood where the sun came through the panes and shone on it.

'Two's company!' he said cheerfully, 'and I'll work all the better for having yours!'

He hadn't been sewing for long when he sneezed, 'Atishoo!' and dropped his needle. He was obliged to go down on the floor and crawl around looking for it. As he was searching, he came upon a spider and her web.

'Alas!' mourned the spider – for that was her kind of conversation. 'My web is torn, and I have no more silk to mend it. Have you a length of fine thread that would serve to sew up the hole?'

'Dear me! That's a nuisance!' answered the tailor. 'But don't worry. I have some mushroom coloured silk which will be exactly the right shade. I will mend it myself, when I find my needle.'

'I shall help you to look,' decided the spider. She scuttled around at a great rate, from one corner to another. She had so many eyes in her head that she could see everything, and it wasn't long before she found a needle.

'How extraordinary!' The tailor took the needle into his hand, and stared at it. 'It's not MY needle. I've never seen this one before. It seems to be made of gold, too, and has a diamond in its eye. Most odd! Most odd! However, I may as well use it, since I have lost my own. Who knows? It may bring us luck!'

And he went on sewing, with the golden needle.

Now, it so happened that a huge, three-headed ogre had come into the land that very day, and was causing an extraordinary amount of damage. He was always hungry. There was never enough for him to eat. He had taken over all the allotments, and swallowed the vegetables . . . he had knocked down the King's stables and snapped them up like biscuits. He had even chewed up the spires of seven churches – exactly as if they had been sticks of liquorice.

'Who will rid me of this terrible three-headed ogre?' cried the King. But no one answered, because they were all afraid. Well, wouldn't YOU have been? I should. Then the King ordered his town cryers to go into every city calling for volunteers to take the three-headed ogre away. I am sorry to say that they only shouted their message out of their bedroom windows, having first locked the doors safely behind them. What could be done with THREE heads? Nothing at all.

The little tailor heard them, as he sat sewing, and wondered how he could help. While he was thinking about things, there was a noise of heavy footsteps – a bit like a train shunting – and a dark shadow fell across the room. Had it not been for the golden needle, he would have not been able to see anything at all; luckily, a beam of

light leaped from the diamond in its eye.

Outside, stood the three-headed ogre.

'Measure me for a suit!' he shouted. 'I need a new one! The suit must have a brooch on the shoulder, and three feathered caps to go with it. All must be finished by midnight, or I shall gobble you up!'

'That's a fine thing!' thought the tailor. 'Why, he is so big, my tape measure will not go round him. I'll have to measure him with the washing line.'

He went outside the back door and took down his washing line . . . but even THAT was not long enough. He had to borrow his neighbour's line, as well, and the one in the garden next to THAT. THREE washing lines just reached round the ogre's waist.

But how would he find enough material?

'Take this!' growled the ogre, and he tossed down a whole roll of curtain material he had stolen from a big store near by. 'And remember,' he added, 'I shall return at midnight. If the suit is not finished, and a brooch and three feathered caps to go with it, I shall gobble you up! Why, you would go down in a single mouthful – just like an oyster!' And he strode off, laughing, 'Ho, ho, ho!'

The tailor set to work without delay, but he believed it would be impossible to finish the garments in time. The curtain material had a pattern of trees and monkeys and parrots. It was difficult to cut out, for he did not want to spoil the design, and you could not have *half* a monkey or *half* a parrot on your trousers. He wanted to make a good job of it, even if it WAS for an ogre – and one with three heads, too. But when it was cut and laid together, the golden needle flew in and out, and the diamond flashed; so that by dusk, the trousers were completed and the jacket half done. By the time the evening star was rising, the golden needle had worked at such a speed that there was little left to do except button holes . . . the caps with feathers in them . . . and the brooch.

He was almost giving up in despair, when a small voice cried out: 'I will do the button holes!' It was the spider whose web he had repaired. In two sniffs, she had them completed. But what about the caps?

'I have brought you three feathers,' squeaked the starling, whose leg he had mended with button thread. 'I heard of your difficulty, and flew here as quickly as I could. Here are the feathers!'

The tailor thanked his friends, and worked on breathlessly. There was not much time left. Now, he had everything but the brooch.

At midnight the sounds of the ogre's footsteps returning were so loud that many people thought there was an earthquake coming:

Thump

THUMP

THUMP

he went, as he came. He was kicking a dustbin in front of him, too, and that made it worse.

'Where's my suit?' he shouted.

'It is quite ready,' answered the tailor, showing it.

'Hmmmm. I'll try it on.'

It fitted perfectly.

'Where are my three caps?'

'They are quite ready,' answered the tailor, bringing the caps with the starling's feathers in them.

'Hmmmm. I'll try them on.'

They all fitted exactly.

'Where's my brooch? If there's no brooch, I shall gobble you up!'

'Here it is,' whispered a tiny voice, and – goodness! An exquisite butterfly was sitting on the ogre's shoulder!

At this, the three-headed ogre was so pleased with his new clothes that he would have invited himself to supper. Fortunately, the tailor's house was much too small for him to go inside. He would certainly have eaten the tables and chairs, and the cooking stove too, I wouldn't wonder.

'You look so splendid,' remarked the tailor, 'that you had better go home immediately to the Land of the Hugies, and show yourself to your friends and relations. They must be wondering where ever you have got to, and may be quite worried.'

So the three-headed ogre went off at once to the Land of the Hugies. He showed all his fine clothes to his friends and relations, and never left home again.

Peace returned to the tailor and his country.

Several days later, there was a faint tapping noise at the window of the tailor's house.

It was the butterfly.

'I flew off,' she whispered softly (for that was her kind of conversation), 'as soon as he had crossed the border into his own place. I spoke to him firmly, before I left him. I told him that if he came back again and started spoiling things, then he would shrink and shrink until he was no bigger than you or me – for his clothes were made by a golden needle.'

'That was perfectly true,' said the tailor thoughtfully. 'A needle with a diamond in its eye isn't found EVERY day.'

And, do you know, after that the needle worked all by itself, without any assistance whatsoever! I suppose it was magic. The tailor sat in his armchair with his feet up. Soon, he became bonnier altogether; his back straightened, and he grew a crop of red, curly hair and a fine moustache to go with it. I have even heard that he became a rich man, and ended up as Lord Mayor of the city, with a peal of bells.

In that country, for ever and ever, it was Sunday afternoon.

And everybody was happy.

Do you believe it?

The Tiger
Who Ate Yeast

Once there was a baker. He lived right at the end of the street where all the shops were, in the village of Stopover. If you came out of his door and turned left, you would pass the butcher and the chemist and the toyshop and the shop that sold magazines and windmills. Then there was the school, with children playing; and opposite, the church. But if you came out of his door and turned right, you would find that the street became narrower and narrower, until it stopped being a street and became a lane. And after it had been a lane for a little time, it became a path. Then it forgot what it was about all together, and wandered over a pretty meadow full of buttercups, crossed a small footbridge, and entered a deep, green, shady forest. Quite soon, it disappeared and was never seen again.

Most of the people visited the baker to buy

their bread, and then turned back again the way they had come. In winter, the village was cheerful with lights and chatter, and the windows glinted and shone. But sometimes, in the summer holiday, when the children were troublesome – or perhaps at Easter when the primroses were coming into flower – small groups would be seen making their way in the opposite direction. They would have quite a different look about them from the look they wore on ordinary days. For one thing, they would be carrying fishing nets, as like as not, and baskets with thermos flasks poking out of the top; some of the grownups would have a towel, in case a child fell over while paddling, and a spare pair of trousers for the boy who *always* tumbled in. They were going on a picnic.

The baker would stand in his doorway and watch them. He liked children, and was pleased when they called in to buy a currant bun or a loaf of new bread. He made the bread himself, and you could smell it cooking in the old bakery at the back of the shop. It smelled delicious. But it was odd, however tightly he packed the shelves, when he came to serve his customers there were always a few gaps. It was exactly as if someone had come in when he wasn't looking, and helped himself.

'But *that* can't be so,' muttered the baker, 'for I should have heard the door bell ring.'

One day, *an entire shelf* was empty. And then he really did begin to get worried. 'Nineteen nutty cobs,' he sighed – 'and not a single one left.'

A robin who was pecking crumbs from the sill gave a sympathetic whistle. 'It's too bad,' he agreed. 'But have you seen the footprints in the flower bed here? ENORMOUS, they are. Someone's been thieving, if you ask me. Some-one with big feet.'

'It was a tiger! It was a tiger!' explained a thrush from the top of the rowan tree. He was proud of being so knowledgable, and repeated himself a great many times. 'It was a tiger! I saw him! It was a tiger!'

The other birds soon got tired of this, and told him to shut up. But the baker listened, and looked very carefully at the footprints over the top of his glasses. Then he measured them with a ruler, and turned up 'tiger' in the encyclopaedia.

The description fitted exactly.

But fancy having a tiger in the village of Stopover! It was unthinkable. Nevertheless, the footprints couldn't be denied. And as the news was passed round, people began to feel nervous, and uncertain, and didn't come to the baker's anything like so often. At last, they didn't come at all.

The baker decided that something must be done.

'I know,' he said. 'I'll follow the footprints, and see where they come from. Perhaps I'll be able to catch the tiger. Or shoot him,' he added rather doubtfully.

He wasn't much good at shooting things.

So one morning, he set off. He took his special stick with him, the one with a swallow carved out of the handle, and a penknife, and a small packet of yeast. You might think it was odd to take yeast on an adventure, but you see he WAS a baker and so it was important, to him. And it was a good thing he DID take it, in the end, as you shall hear . . .

The baker turned right, out of his shop, and followed the road till it became a lane. Then he crossed a stile, for the footprints were apparent on both sides of it, and went on . . . The river ran right through the middle of a meadow, but there were no marks on the bridge that made you think of tigers; none at all. The steps just went up the bank, the other side.

'Must have *swum* over,' settled the baker. And he asked the swan, who was sailing down stream very proudly with his wings up-ended and all blown out like a sugar meringue.

'Have YOU seen a tiger, this way?'

'I *did* see a stripy creature with no feathers paddling over in the shallows,' admitted the swan. 'But I didn't pay much attention. I was anxious to keep my wife and family out of his way. I ordered them to remain below the bridge until he had gone; and they did so, for they are always obedient. Nevertheless, there was a great deal of commotion among the rushes. And he has planted his clumsy foot on the side of my nesting place – only see how the twigs are tumbled! It will take a long time to straighten them again. You can help me, if you wish.'

The baker thought the swan a grand creature. 'He talks like a king,' he said to himself, and he spent a little while building up the nest again to suit the swan's requirements.

'The stripy creature went off in THAT direction,' volunteered the swan, sweeping proudly upstream to collect his family. 'Over *there*. Where the forest is. We do not go into the forest. It is dark; and I believe it is dangerous. Goodbye.'

He swam off, pushing strongly with his black, webbed feet, and leaving a V-shaped pattern on the water behind him.

So the baker walked on; and when he had

crossed the bridge he found it quite easy to pick up the trail.

It did go into the forest.

At first, it was pleasant to be out of the heat of the meadow, and shaded from the bright glare of the sun. But as the trees grew more closely, it became darker and darker, and soon it was hard to see what was a tree and what wasn't. So when he came upon the tiger, stretched out on a log with his tail one end and his whiskers another, it quite made him jump. He had to sit down for a minute, and think things over.

The tiger opened one eye.

'And who might YOU be?' he enquired sleepily, thwacking his tail against the side of the log.

'I am the b . . . b . . . baker. You stole my b . . . b . . . bread. I have come to ask you not to venture into the village any more.'

The tiger yawned, hugely. He had a great many teeth, and they glinted, whitely, in a hungry sort of way.

'B . . . b . . . baker?' he mocked. 'B . . . b . . . bread? But I LIKE bread. It's very GOOD bread. Have you brought some with you?'

('This isn't getting very far,' thought the baker. 'I must try cunning.) I have a suggestion to make,' he went on. 'Let us have a competition. If

you win, then I will allow you twenty loaves every morning. But if *I* win, then you must promise never to steal my bread again.'

'Why should I promise?' jeered the tiger. 'I don't bother with competitions. I can help myself to your bread whenever I please.'

'Ah,' replied the baker, 'that is true. But it will not always be so easy. Already the town policeman knows about you, and if you continue with your thieving he will turn out with the whole police force, and the Salvation Army too, and catch you in a net. Then they will put you in a zoo, and you will not be free to wander where you choose any more. You will have to eat peanuts, and be stared at.'

The tiger looked a little anxious. 'What IS

your competition, then?' he questioned.

'Each of us must ask the other a riddle. Like this,' explained the baker. 'What rises at the same time as it sets?'

The tiger thought. He thought for a long time, and gnawed his front paw.

'I give up,' he said sulkily.

'A good *loaf*, of course. Now it's *your* turn.'

It took the tiger a lot of pacing to and fro before a riddle came slowly up into his head. 'What has eyes, yet cannot see?' he asked furtively, scratching his ear.

'A butterfly?'

'No.'

'It has, you know. It has eyes painted on its wings,' pointed out the baker.

'That's not the answer I meant.'

'A surpr-*ise*, then?'

'Yeeees! Bother!'

The tiger was angry that his riddle had been guessed. It was not a very GOOD riddle. He stretched himself, and walked round and round the baker, looking at him scornfully and making the middle part of his eye very black and the outside part of it very yellow. 'You think you can persuade me, I suppose,' he scoffed. 'Don't you know that nobody can persuade me to do ANYTHING I don't want to do? Why should I stay in the forest, anyway? I get tired of it, sometimes. Now,' (he lashed his tail savagely, and stretched his claws), 'what we really should have is a wrestling match. Riddles are stOOPID. I'll walk *this* way, you walk *that* way, and when we meet, we'll fight. GRRRRRRR!'

He began circling the log, and the baker stood still. At least, he would have been still if his teeth had not been chattering. He shook so much that the packet of yeast fell out of his pocket . . . it burst open, and the yeast scattered . . .

The Tiger stopped.

He tasted a bit.

He licked a bit.

He made comfortable noises, and swallowed a huge mouthful . . .

Soon, there was no yeast left at all.

But – what a PECULIAR feeling! He felt himself swaying with an odd sort of lightness, blowing this way and that . . . his feet hardly touched the ground. *The yeast had made him rise, just like a loaf of bread*! He rose, and he rose and he rose.

'Help!' called the tiger. 'I can't walk! I can only float! Help! I'm turning into a balloon!'

'Wait!' shouted the baker. He reached up with his stick (the one that had a swallow carved out of the handle) and pulled down a strand of ivy. He cut a length of it with his penknife. It is always useful to have a penknife and a stick. When he had snipped off a piece about two metres long, he made a noose in one end of it, and swung it three times round his head – just like a lassoo.

Whoosh!

Whoosh!

Whoosh!

And then –

CAUGHT!

The loop fell neatly over the tiger's head.

'Whew! That was a near one! I nearly floated away altogether!'

'It serves you right for stealing other people's yeast,' reprimanded the baker. 'What next? It's bad enough when the bread is stolen, but when you eat my YEAST as well, then I have no alternative but to take you to prison. However, I am a *kind* man, and if you will promise to help me now and again in my bakery, I will let you come home with me. Floating or walking – it's all one to me.'

He tucked the other end of the ivy securely in his belt, and set off on his homeward journey through the forest. The tiger followed behind, bouncing delicately from bough to bough, and sometimes floating airily among the branches. He looked more like a parrot than a tiger, and not

anything like so fierce, up there. When he growled, it was a very *small* growl, all high and squeaky.

Like this – grrrrrrrr.

When they reached the river, the swan was just passing with his wife and family behind him.

'Caught him?' he enquired. 'A flying tiger, eh?

Nasty, rough fellow. Common, with all those stripes. Keep away from my nesting site, old chap, will you?'

He sailed grandly on.

In the meadow, a group of children were gathering buttercups. 'Cor! Look at that! A flying tiger! You ever seen a flying tiger?'

And they all followed after the baker, so that there was quite a large procession; and at the end of it, a very small boy indeed, who wanted to put the tiger in his jam jar.

At last they reached the baker's shop. The door stood open, and there was nothing on the shelves at all except a custard pie.

'You see?' complained the baker. 'They don't come any more, so I don't make any bread, except nutty cobs. And YOU eat them. Don't you!' he threatened.

'Won't do it again,' promised the tiger, meekly. 'Not ever. Only tell me how to walk about in an ordinary manner, like an ordinary tiger. Only tell me that, and I'll give up eating bread and take to radishes.'

'Exercise will help,' the baker told him severely. 'Suppose you assist me in the bakery. Suppose you help me knead the bread, and put the loaves in the oven. Then we'll see what happens.'

So the tiger promised that he would help.

The baker put him to bed in the dog kennel, and tied the ivy firmly to a large stone, so that he shouldn't blow away. And morning after morning, wet, fine or frosty, the baker and the tiger shut themselves up in the bakery and kneaded bread. The tiger had strong, muscular front legs, and large paws just the right shape for pummelling. He pushed and he pulled, he thumped and he twisted. Then they put the dough to rise; and it rose and it rose and it rose so that the loaves came out of the oven three times as large as they used to be, and all crispy and sweet on top. Before many weeks had passed, people started to come to the shop again. First, they came in ones and twos, and then in groups and parties; and soon there were long queues of them stretching right down the High Street.

The baker started a delivery round. He made a handsome cart, and asked the tiger if he would pull it. The tiger had grown so good-natured that he said he would. Every Tuesday and every Thursday the pair of them went round the village, delivering bread to people who were too old or too busy to fetch it for themselves. And at every round, the tiger felt his feet to be more firmly on the ground, until at last he really was as ordinary as anything.

By then, he had grown so fond of the baker

that he did not want to leave him. He did not want to go back into the darkness of the forest.

The two of them settled down together, and became the best of friends. If there was ever any bread left over, the baker would make bread puddings, and the tiger would eat one half of the dish while his friend ate the other half.

In the end, even the name over the shop door was altered. It did not say:

BAKER,

Nutty Cobs and Doughnuts

any more. It said:

At Christmas, there was a decorated tree outside, as tall as Salisbury Cathedral. Or very nearly.

I believe it, anyway. Do you?

Tiger

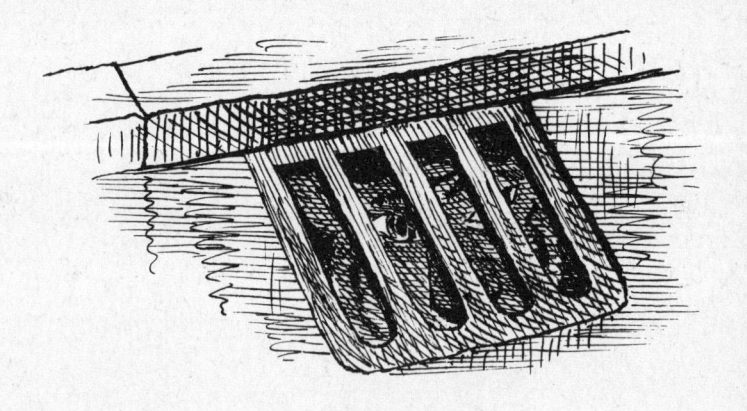

Down by the Market Place
  Over the motorway
     half way along
       shiny Scudamore Street
There's a drain in the gutter
  with bars fixed across it
     and darkness inside of it
      secret and deep.

I don't know what's in there.
  They say that rain water
     and leaves, and old rubbish
      are all that is found –
But there may be a tiger
  escaped from the jungle.
     There may be a tiger
      who's gone underground.

The Hotchpotch Horse

So when I am crossing
   the bridge on the motorway,
         half way along
               shiny Scudamore Street
I walk very gingerly,
   being especially
      careful of where
            I am putting my feet.

You can't believe everything
   people keep telling you –
         can't believe everything
               other folk say . . .
There may be a tiger
   ferocious and splendid
         who's down in the dust and the rubbish
               today!

Magic and Peculiarities

There was once a wizard, who became tired of living in the Land of Magic and Peculiarity and decided to set up house in an ordinary village among ordinary folk. So that is what he did; and some years ago quite early in the morning – I believe it was soon after nine o'clock, for the church clock had just ceased striking – he appeared in the High Street of Little Mudby.

Now Little Mudby was a friendly village. It wasn't very large. There was a school, a church, a house with a brass plate outside saying DOCTOR, and a straggle of shops selling things like doughnuts, bootlaces, forks for digging the garden, toffee apples and knicker elastic. The last shop was empty, and here the wizard decided to settle. It was quite easy to enter, for the doors were open; locks do not stay firm when there is magic around. Soon, the window held a nice display of wares: spells, charms, incantations, riddle-me-rees, TRANSFORMATIONS in twopenny packets, and invisible snakes for fourpence. Why, there was even a selection of tall hats for sale. But they were expensive; at least twenty pence each. People passing by, with their shopping baskets in one hand and a list in the other, paused, and pressed their faces to the pane. One or two ventured inside. Cures for toothache were cheap; tricks for passing examinations would make useful gifts . . . It wasn't long before the wizard and his wares became widely known, and a brand new notice in strange lettering appeared hung over the entrance:

MAGIC AND PECULIARITIES, it said.

It so happened that at the end of the High Street was a school playground with swings, slides, tubes, tunnels, climbing frames, and all sorts of exciting things in it. There was a bin, too, for putting rubbish in – and behind it, darkly hidden in a patch of stinging nettles – lived a fierce and dreadful witch. Not all witches are fierce and dreadful, you must know. Some of them are kind and helpful, and use their gifts to set things right. But Stinging Nancy was a real baddie. You could guess that she was there from the way the rubbish bin was tipped over from time to time, and the cans and cartons scattered over the playground. Then, footballs and quoits, balloons and kites and marbles, had a habit of disappearing into the nettles.

They were never found again. Children who searched for a lost toy would cry out that they had been badly stung, and run to the other end of the playground to rub themselves with dock leaves. That's how things were.

Stinging Nancy had lived for so long that she had forgotten in what year she had been born. Was she five hundred years old? Or a thousand? More than that? She celebrated a birthday whenever she felt like it: usually on Friday afternoons when the weathermen had prophesied a wet weekend and there was a reliable drizzle, with a cutting east wind that bit through it at every corner. She didn't like sunshine, you see. She had lived in darkness for so long, that any sort of light made her eyes run. But when she heard from a passing magpie that there was a shop selling magic and peculiarities in the village, she made up her mind that she must nip out and visit it without delay.

So nip out she did, though not until nearly closing time. She did not want anyone to see her, you can be sure of that. For the funny thing was, although she was up to all sorts of tricks and trades, and could send people bad dreams a-plenty, Stinging Nancy had never learned to make herself wholly invisible. Only partly so. Sometimes, when she scurried across the playground, a boy might catch sight of her tall, steeple hat, or the glint of a black eye, or even a finger nail, as green as bottle-glass. On these occasions the boy would cry out: 'I can see Stinging Nancy!' in as loud a voice as he could muster. Then the school mistress would hasten to light a candle, (she kept a bundle of them under her desk lid) and Stinging Nancy would groan and grumble and scuttle back to her own private darkness. Light was the worst thing in the world for her.

Well, on that winter afternoon the shops closed as dusk fell, and nobody noticed Stinging Nancy creeping and sliding from door to door, her back pressed against the wall, and her tall hat casting steeple shadows. It wasn't long before she reached the shop selling magic and peculiarities. The wizard was rearranging his window with a most tempting array of new stock. There were shiny balls of crystal for gazing into, so that you could see what was going to happen to you in the future. There were potions to make people fall in love, and potions to help them fall out again when things became uncomfortable. There were trampolines that would send you into Pixieland and back twice daily on a cheap ticket, bags of powder paints for turning your hair all the colours of the rainbow, and spectacles with rose-tinted lenses.

The wizard sang, under his breath, as he put out his stock, drawing back to look at it every now and then with his head on one side.

> *'Who would – who would like to see*
> *Some PECULIARITY?*
> *When you're out a-walking – stop!*
> *Spend a moment in my shop.*
> *Everything is labelled clearly*
> *(Though, you may think, rather queerly!),*
> *All are magic goods which I*
> *Have to offer. Buy! Come, buy!'*

Stinging Nancy rubbed her nose up and down the pane, to make a clear circle to stare through. Then she drew in her breath, whwhwhew! There was a tiny box in the window. Red, it was, with a small, slightly twisted, brass handle.

'That'll be a musical box, I'll swear!' cackled Stinging Nancy.

'Care for a tune?' called the wizard. He could see there was *somebody* looking through the window, though it was difficult to tell quite WHO.

Stinging Nancy drew herself up so that she

was about six feet in height, and as she did so her shadow darkened yet again and became as narrow as a carving knife.

'Play! Play!' she commanded.

The wizard put his fingers to the handle, and turned. What a pretty tune! Light and delicate as a butterfly in the meadow. He stopped.

'Play some WRONG notes,' wheedled Stinging Nancy. 'The wrrrrrong ones are bessst.'

But the wizard answered that he hadn't got any wrong notes – only right ones. He turned the handle again, and the tune changed. It became a dance. How merry it was, too! Even a bus conductor would have kicked up his legs, had he heard it.

'I don't think much of the tunes,' muttered Stinging Nancy. 'They're too happy. But I dare say I could alter that, with a little experiment. How much for the musical box?' she whined. 'A bit of silver? A bit of tin?'

'Neither tin nor silver can buy the box,' said the wizard. 'It is my special treasure and plays only my special tunes. It would be of no use to you, or anyone else. It is not for sale.'

At that, Stinging Nancy grew suddenly bad-tempered.

'Invisible snakes, then,' she snapped. 'Give me four penn'orth. Four penn'orth of invisible snakes, and I hope they bite.'

The wizard dropped the fourpence into his box, and carried away a bunch of invisible snakes to wrap them up in tissue paper. That is the best thing to do with things that are invisible; otherwise, one might very quickly lose them. Stinging Nancy tucked the packet under her tall hat, and sneaked off. But as soon as she had heard the door shut behind her, she hid under the porch.

Then, when the wizard had disappeared into the inner room to add up his profits, she stretched one long, skinny arm, one brown, spidery hand, through the letter slit, and snatched the red musical box.

Very, very carefully she withdrew it.

'Got it!' she whispered horribly, and fled.

If you had been in the school playground that night you would have heard some curious and unpleasant noises coming from the patch of nettles behind the rubbish bin. However quickly or slowly Stinging Nancy turned the handle, the tunes came out differently than before; in fact, they weren't dances at all, but what seemed to be an ancient, croaky old jumble of bangs, bumps, squeals, scratches and screeches – rather as if a band of saws and stones and saucepan lids were all fighting together. Stinging Nancy grew crosser and crosser. She took the musical box to pieces, and chanted spells over the tiny screws and springs and hammers. Some of them were so minute that they got lost under the nettles, and she had the greatest difficulty in finding them again. Three times she took it apart, three times she fixed it together again, having recited every one of the ninety and nine spells of darkness. But none of them made any difference, and soon the noise and disturbance was so great that quite a gathering of creatures crept up to the tangled patch behind the rubbish bin to see what was happening.

> *'Witchy witchy what-not,*
> *Witchy witchy wops –*
> *Who steals music*
> *Out of shops?'*

sniggered a fox.

> *'The bogie will get you*
> *If you don't watch out!'*

screamed a blackbird.

> *'If you put a spell in*
> *I'm telling! I'm telling!'*

warned a thrush who had several times only just escaped being trapped by Stinging Nancy and fried for her supper.

By that time, dawn had broken and the sun was beginning to rise. It was a wintry sun, more silver than golden, but who cared for that? Gradually, a great ball of light shone over the playground, and was reflected in every drop of dew, so that each one glittered with a diamond brightness.

That is the sort of thing to bring an end to black magic. Stinging Nancy threw the musical box furiously into the dustbin, and tumbled head first after it. Her hat slid off – and the invisible snakes went with it. So when the refuse collectors came round a few hours later, and emptied the bins into their lorry, weren't they surprised at what they found?

'Cor! Look at this 'ere, Alf!' cried one to his mate. 'A musical box, ain't it?'

'A musical box it is,' agreed Alf, scratching his head in bewilderment. 'But it'll be broken, most likely. Turn the 'andle, Albert. Let's try for a tune.'

Albert wiped his hands on the seat of his trousers, for they were rather oily, and began, rather doubtfully, to turn the knob. A thin, high tumble of bells came first. Then the music – how it danced! One tune came tripping after another, and Alf and Albert were soon tapping their toes to keep time. Many people wondered why the refuse collectors were dancing down the road with their rubbish bins.

'Something must have happened,' they decided. 'A coronation? Or maybe it's their birthday. Maybe they're twins?' Certainly, once the music had begun, nothing could stop it.

And Stinging Nancy? She had shrunk so small she appeared no bigger than a tatter of dark rags – and had soon disappeared completely beneath a pile of old gas stoves and broken buckets on the tip. I think myself the invisible snakes had something to do with it. Snakes are clever. They might have built a snake pit under all that rubbish, and made quite sure that Stinging Nancy never escaped again. They were invisible, you see, and were up to all sorts of games and fancies. But they didn't bite. They were MUCH too clever for that.

The musical box played its dances for a whole day; and then, it gave a sort of click and stopped. Alf and Albert tried to mend it, but although they oiled the little springs and wheels most carefully, and turned the handle again and again – not a tune came out. Only a hiccup. So they took it to the wizard who was re-arranging his magic and peculiarities window, and singing quietly to himself:

> '*Who would – who would like to see*
> *Some peculiarity?*'

He was so delighted to get the musical box back that he gave them each a free ticket for a trip to Pixieland and back.

You can imagine how they enjoyed THAT!

The musical box is with the same owner today, for the wizard will not sell it.

'It plays MY tunes best,' he explained. 'Everyone has his own tune. But not everybody knows it.'

If you ever find yourself visiting Little Mudby, look out for a shop with the name MAGIC AND PECULIARITIES. There will be all sorts of interesting things in the window.

And there, if I'm not mistaken, you will find it.

The
Snow-Baby

A boy looked out of the window. It was snowing. Yes, it WAS snowing – make no mistake about that. The air was filled with a strange, unusual brightness; and even the postman's footsteps were thickly muffled as if he were shod with fur.

The boy breathed on the glass, and then pressed his nose into the circle he had made.

'I'll build a snowman,' he whispered. 'I'll build one now, before anyone's about.'

He dressed quickly, and stood at the back door, shaking a spider out of his wellies. He took a step, and then another. Cor! It was deep. Twenty centimetres? And more, where the wind had shuffled it into peaks and mountains.

He picked up a handful and pressed it hard, between his palms. Then he rolled the ball a little way, and a little way again, and yet again. It grew and grew. A golf ball . . . a cricket ball . . . a football . . . at last, it was up to his waist, and he had to lean over and put his shoulder to it to get it to move at all.

The boy became red, and hot. He took off his scarf, and stood back, panting.

'That'll do for his body,' he said.

He rolled another ball, but not quite so big as the first one.

'That'll do for his head.'

He collected two round pebbles for eyes, a curved twig for a mouth. An old tin, upside down, made a top hat. A fallen branch made a walking stick.

So . . . it was finished. And it was nearly dinner-time. The boy stamped his feet to get the snow off, and shook himself. He was proud of his work, and looked back over his shoulder at it, as he went up the path to the house; at least, he supposed it was the path, because he had walked that way so many times, but it had disappeared and there was nothing to show where the lawn ended and the garden began.

The door closed. The boy had gone.

Outside, the snowman very slowly winked a pebble eye . . .

The next day, the snow ceased falling and in the blue sky the sun shone, as round as an egg.

Everything glittered. The boy moulded two arms, and pressed them into the snowman's side. At first they fell off and crumbled, but then they stayed, and for hands he gave him a pair of woolly mittens.

And again, when the boy went indoors at evening, the snowman winked a pebble eye.

At bedtime, the boy twitched back his curtain and peered out. He looks lonely, he thought, standing out there in the snow. He needs company. Tomorrow I'll build a snow-lady.

He did. A big ball for the body, a little ball for the head, two eyes, a nose and a mouth. There wasn't another tin about, so the boy dressed the snow-lady in a paper hat left over from Christmas. It was made of pink tissue, with yellow stars on it, and he tied it under her chin. To keep her arms in place, he fixed a muff, that was a worn sock with a hole in it.

Then the game was finished. The boy forgot about the snow-people, and went sledging.

And again it snowed.

That night, a great icicle formed on the edge of the snowman's mittens. It dripped on to the snow-lady's muff, and froze hard. They were holding hands.

Very slowly, very tentatively, they began to come alive.

At first, they had breathing difficulties because they were so cold, but they soon got into the way of it: in, out . . . in, out. Then they moved a little . . . a muscle here . . . a muscle there. The snow-lady wrinkled her nose. The snowman sniffed.

'Now, my dear,' he said in husky tones as if the snow were inside as well as outside of him. 'It's time we had a house. We should move into a safe place, before the thaw comes. We should get out of the way of the sun.'

At the word 'sun' the snow-lady paled, and shivered.

'Let's go, Charlie,' she entreated. 'Let's go *now*. I can walk. I know I can, if I try.'

'Hold on to my arm,' whispered Charlie. 'We'll dodge . . . before the moon comes up. So's THEY won't see us.'

'What'll we do if they do, Charlie?' asked the snow-lady anxiously.

'We'll run. And if the worst comes to the worst – we can melt. No human bein' can catch us then. They don't understand melting, Emmeline. We must all melt some day. But they don't understand.'

Arm in arm, the snow-people rambled off. They moved with a sort of bumping motion, as if they were in a sack race, for you see they hadn't any proper feet. But they made good progress, and decided to set up house in the gardening shed. First, they cut the window larger. Then they sawed holes in the roof, because snow-people have to be able to see the sky – or else they feel faint.

'Plenty of draught! Plenty of draught!' hummed Charlie. He rather fancied himself as a handyman. There were hammers and screwdrivers in the shed, and he used them cleverly though he could not remove his mittens for fear his hands might drop off.

'You need TWO pairs, Charlie,' said Emmeline, and she made him a second pair out of some raffia she had found on a hook. 'That means there'll be one for the wash.'

All that winter the snow-people lived in the gardening shed, and nobody knew they were there. But when spring came, and it was time to prepare the ground and plant seeds, THEY started coming into the shed at odd moments, for a fork, or a couple of nails, or a piece of string. The snow-people squeezed themselves into a corner on these occasions. It was possible when there were only two of them. But what would happen when their snow-baby was born? What if they should be discovered?

The snow-baby arrived in March. It was very

small, about as big as a coconut, and because it is not easy to tell whether snow-people are going to be boys or girls when they are tiny, they called it Peppercorn.

'That will do for either,' they said.

There was plenty of good food in the shed: tintacks, and rawlplugs, bits of putty, even fragments of sellotape. 'Much better than anything *I* had when I was a boy,' remonstrated Charlie, when Peppercorn was stuffing himself with screws. 'More body-building. You don't need so much. You don't want to grow HARD, child, do you?'

Charlie was getting old, and Emmeline noticed that he was beginning to melt a bit at the edges, but she did not like to mention it.

But although, as the weather became warmer, she and Charlie became smaller and smaller and thinner and thinner and weaker and weaker, Peppercorn seemed to thrive on the early sunshine; and one night he dreamed of summer.

'You dreamed of WHAT?' asked Emmeline, anxiously.

'Of summer, Ma.'

'That's a wicked word! A wicked word! Never let me hear you use it again. Not in this house.'

'You're getting too big for your snowboots, Pep,' warned Charlie. 'Snow-people do not stay through the summer. It is our going time,' he explained softly, 'only it seems like dying to those who do not understand. THEY think we don't survive, when we return to water. Of course, they're wrong.'

'They?' queried Peppercorn.

'The H.B.'s. Human bein's, see? They think we're finished. But we ain't.'

'What happens, then?'

'Ah! That's a secret I'm not telling. Not till you're older, and you know the difference between Something and Other.'

He sighed. A large drop fell from his nose. He would not last much longer.

The first of May came, bright and shiny. On the banks, celandine and violets were out, and primroses. Emmeline and Charlie had stayed until Easter morning; then, without leaving a message, they had disappeared. Only a damp patch on the floor showed where they had stood.

Peppercorn was big enough to look after himself, by then. He was full of tintacks and nuts and bolts, and was proud of his hard strength. Only the fiercest flame would be able to destroy him. But he was foolhardy, and had never taken any advice.

'Keep away from the fire, Peppercorn,' Emmeline had whispered hastily, the evening before she went. 'Especially on Bonfire night. You may not be so strong as you think . . .'

'Pooh!' he had replied; and the next morning he had run five times round the garden, rattling, to show that he would not melt however hot he grew.

He became bolder and bolder. Once, he even jumped out of the shed when a H.B. was around.

'Get out!' he bawled. 'This is MY shed!'

'It isn't, you know,' answered the H.B. testily. 'And I'll toast you if I catch you – watch out!'

But Peppercorn was nimble, and nobody DID catch him. He sang, as he hopped around:

'Up and down the country,
As far as you can see,
There's no snow-baby
Cleverer than me!
Up and down the country . . .'

'Shut up!' snapped a rat who lived under the floorboards. 'You'll have a fall, one of these days. You've too much pride. Too many tin-tacks . . . you're greedy.'

But Peppercorn went on singing.

The summer passed, and autumn came on. It was dull in the gardening shed, without Emmeline and Charlie. On Bonfire night Peppercorn could not resist creeping out to join the children's party round the burning branches.

'Hooray!' they cried, as rocket after rocket surged up into the night sky.

'Hooray!' cried Peppercorn. He ran, skipped and gambolled with the others. Nobody noticed him. Then, he drew close to a rocket, and put his fingers on the stick . . .

'Keep back!' called an H.B. 'Look out! It's just going off! It's dangerous!'

Too late . . .

With a spurt and a splutter, the rocket shot up

into the dark distance, carrying Peppercorn with it. Higher and higher and higher yet it soared, till even the stars seemed to be left behind, and the earth itself was a small, round bubble far below.

Then it exploded into a cascade of coloured light.

'I'm flying!' cried Peppercorn. 'Look at me! Look!

> *Up and down the country*
> *As far as you can see,*
> *There's no snow-baby . . .'*

His voice faded.

He fell down . . .

Down . . .

Down . . .

till he landed in the fish pool at the bottom of the garden.

Splosh!

That was nasty. There were frogs in the pool. Peppercorn was heavy. He didn't feel quite so sure of himself in water. With all that iron inside him, it was really difficult to swim. At last, he managed to drag himself on to a stone; and there he shook and shivered till his innards rattled.

There were human bein's about. It would be wisest to keep still.

Clenching his teeth to stop them chattering, he kept so still you might have thought he was only a sort of gnome made of nails and oddments, just pretending, perhaps, to be a statue. When the human bein's drew nearer they expressed astonishment, for they had never seen a statue in the pond before and they wondered how it had arrived and where it had come from. One by one they marvelled, and went away.

But Peppercorn was spellbound. He had forgotten . . . what had he NOT forgotten? It's my belief he had forgotten all he had ever learned. He was . . . he was almost a THING. And he wasn't breathing any more, either.

A few days later, there came a spell of bitter weather. Snow fell, covering the garden with a soft, thick blanket. To Peppercorn, it felt strangely familiar. The snow clung to him gently, persistently. It seeped into his very inside. His throat became husky, too, as if the cold were travelling down it. He tried to move, but could not, for the surface of the pond had turned to ice and gripped him tightly. He had forgotten his song. He remembered only the sweetness of the falling snow . . . It was as though Emmeline and Charlie were not far away, after all, but had returned and were very near to him.

Then the boy came down the path in his

wellies, stopped, and looked at Peppercorn.

'Funny!' he remarked. 'That's just like the snow-people I made last year – but smaller. The ones that disappeared. We never *did* find where they had got to.'

He touched Peppercorn, gently.

'He must be lonely, all by himself,' said the boy. 'I'll build a snow-lady, tomorrow, to keep him company. Then there'll be two.'

And he did.

The
Magic Sovereign

A man and his wife once lived in the middle of a large village. Their house was a terraced one, which means that it was joined, on both sides, to others. It was small, having only one room upstairs and one down, for they had no children and were not rich. Outside, you could see coal mines, and slag heaps, and men going to work at different times of day . . . returning later with black smudges of coal on their faces. But the man in my story was not a miner. He was a road mender. It was his job to drive a special lorry which had a great tub of tar at the back of it, and a sack full of tiny, sharp flints. When he came to a hole in the road he would stop, and, jumping out, he would fill the hole neatly and then layer it with tar, and tiny stones, which would set hard and smooth. He was proud of these hard, smooth places, and thought that the road looked as good as new when he had mended it. He worked by himself, too, and he liked that, for he was a solitary person and dreamed dreams.

One hot, summer's day, when he had been working since early morning and was tired, and sticky with sweat, he drew up wearily beside a strange crevice in the road. It was narrow, but seemed unusually deep; a car or bicycle coming upon it suddenly might twist its wheel and suffer a severe accident. The man got out of his lorry, and began to fill the gap. But no matter how big a shovelful of earth he tipped into the hole, it never touched the bottom, but disappeared out of sight.

'It must be VERY deep,' he said to himself, after he had been working for an hour or more. 'Perhaps it reaches to the centre of the earth? Or to Australia?' He went on filling it in until dusk, but whatever he did appeared to make no differ-ence. At last, he poured his final sack of sharp, gritty stones into the hole, revved up his engine, and went home.

'I'll come again tomorrow,' he told himself. 'I'll bring MORE stones – two or three sacks – and flatten the flints with tar. That should do the trick.'

Then he ate a plate of baked beans and fish fingers, for that was his favourite meal, and went to bed, limping a little, because his feet ached.

The next day he started early and loaded on to his lorry as many sacks of flints as it could carry. He was anxious to finish the job as soon as possible, and move on. But the same thing happened as yesterday. No matter how much earth, or how many stones, were poured into the crevice, they never reached either bottom or top. The man began to despair.

Suddenly, just as he was preparing to drive off and fetch still MORE, his eye was caught by a glitter of gold.

What was it?

Something seemed to be stuck under a rim of pebbles. A jewel? A ring? He leaned over, reached down, and gave it a tug.

It was a thin – a very thin – gold coin.

'That's funny,' said the man, looking at it closely. 'It's not a coin as belongs to this country. Why, that's not our Queen's head that's on it. I'd better take it to the bank, and find out what's what.'

So he hopped on to his lorry, and rattled along with the coin in his pocket wrapped in a bit of paper he had found near it. After all, it was not any larger than a tiddly-wink, and might easily have got lost.

There was a queue of people at the bank, each waiting for his turn, so the man joined it and took the coin out of his pocket to inspect it again while he was waiting.

What was his astonishment to find the bit of paper in which it was wrapped covered with tiny writing! It was SO tiny, that it was only by borrowing a magnifying glass from one of the clerks that he was able to read it at all.

This is what it said:

Road mender, when you come back,
Do not try to fill our crack! –
Never spill on us a sack –

Then you will not lose, or lack!
But if you our secret sell,
Nothing, nothing will go well . . .
Do not, do not, do not tell
Where the faerie sovereign fell!

The note was written in pale, greenish ink, and as soon as he had read it the words disappeared completely, and the paper was empty.

'No good explaining THAT to the bank manager,' thought the man to himself. 'He'll think I'm making it up. But I'll ask him what country the coin comes from. There'll be no harm in that.'

So he enquired. The bank manager held the coin up to the light between finger and thumb.

'It's got strange signs on it,' he murmured, 'Not our language – not our language at all! And this head on the back – it's peculiar. It keeps changing shape. First it's a man, then it's a woman. Now, look! It's like nothing so much as a lizard, after all! You'd be wise to throw it away. It can't be REAL gold.'

He was anxious to get rid of the coin, and give his attention to another customer, who would want advice about ORDINARY money. He knew a GREAT deal about THAT, you may be certain.

The road mender wrapped up the coin in paper once more, and putting it safely in his pocket, he went home.

That night, he discussed the whole matter with his wife, as she sat on the other side of the fireplace, knitting bedsocks ready for the winter.

'You've been dreaming, husband – dreaming again,' she told him. 'It's probably a child's bit of pretend money, that's all. A child would have dropped it see, and forgotten all about it. I don't believe in magic, myself.'

The man was disappointed. 'It was funny about the writing, wasn't it?' he suggested. 'The pale, greeny ink? And the way it came and went?'

'I'VE never seen such ink,' said his wife impatiently. 'That's what I call rubbish.'

It was true that the bit of paper had been empty of words when he had showed it to her. But when he had held it up before the mirror, while she was out of the room, the rhyme appeared as clearly as before. It was the same message, but there were only two lines of it this time, and in back-to-front mirror writing:

Do not, do not, do not tell
Where the faerie sovereign fell!

He put the coin carefully in a vase which stood

on the mantelshelf. There were drawing pins and matchsticks and pipe cleaners and paper clips in the vase. The coin wriggled a little, like a goldfish. It slid down among the oddments, and was quickly out of sight.

For the rest of that summer, things went surprisingly well for the road mender. For one thing, he didn't have his usual attack of hay fever. Why, he never sneezed once, not even when harvesters were cutting the hay. The holes which he had filled in had been pointed out to the local council, who sent a representative to inspect them. He was so impressed with the smoothness of the roads that he gave the road mender a new lorry, with a musical windscreen-wiper that played tunes, and a special pair of overalls so that he wouldn't have to spoil his trousers with splashes of tar any more. His wages were increased, too. They were able to buy ice-creams quite often – the biggest cornets, with spikes of chocolate stuck in them.

Then the man's wife began to get restless. First she wanted this, then that. She bought an expensive chair for her husband to sit in when he came home from work; but he didn't like it so much as the old rocker and sent it back to the shop. The road mender liked old things best – especially if they rocked, because then you could dream when you were sitting in them. He enjoyed dreaming.

One morning, a salesman came to the door asking for pieces of old china, and giving new, cheap ornaments in exchange.

'Any old china? Any old china?' he whined, as he stood with one foot inside the door, his beady eyes shifting round the room. 'What about that vase on the mantelshelf?' he begged. 'I'll give you fivepence for it. Five pence, and a cut-glass vinegar bottle.' He knew the vase had a treasure in it, for he was gifted with second sight, and could see the inside as well as the outside of things. Alas, he made wicked use of his gift!

The wife admired the glass vinegar bottle, for she had not much judgement, and decided that the exchange would be a good one. She quickly handed the vase over. 'You'd best be off before my husband comes home,' she warned the salesman, 'for he's a man who prefers old to new, and dreams to common sense.'

The salesman hurried off with his prize.

That night, the road mender noticed a glass vinegar bottle on the mantelshelf where the old vase with all its contents had been.

'You silly woman!' he cried. 'You have let the golden coin go with it!'

'And what use was that?' she scoffed.

'I can tell you one thing,' sighed her husband. 'It was the coin that brought us our good luck. NOW, who knows what may happen?'

The woman would not believe him. But the next morning she upset the kettle and scalded herself as she was making tea. Then, she tripped over the coal scuttle and sprained her ankle. So you can see that things were not going so well. The fire would not burn, either, nor the bread rise, nor the washing dry – and the porridge stuck to the pan. At last, the house was in such a state that the road mender announced he would have to chase after the salesman and ask him to return the sovereign. He hoped that he would not have gone far.

'For what's magic may not be sold or bartered,' he told his wife, and started off walking quickly, one foot before the other, since he wanted to catch up with the salesman before nightfall and his petrol tank was empty.

It was noon by the time he reached the crevice in the road, that no amount of stones could fill. The salesman was sitting on a stile beside it, eating bread and bacon and swinging his legs. No sooner did he catch sight of the road mender than he leaped down, and began to run – for he had many stolen things about him, and was inclined to be light-fingered. As he ran, he

tripped on a pebble, tottered, and tumbled head-long into the crevice . . . down . . . down . . . down . . . down . . . down . . . whooooo!

The road mender lay on his stomach and peered in, but he could see nothing.

Nothing at all.

He called – but there was no answer; only a faint, distant echo of his own voice. As he listened, out of the corner of his eye he saw – or *thought* he saw – a tiny, green figure leaping exultantly in the darkness far below, and holding between its diminutive finger and thumb what appeared to be a thin, gold coin. It wasn't as big as ordinary human money, but lighter – rather like a tiddly-wink, in fact.

It was the missing sovereign.

In a minute, or less, that, too, had vanished.

Next day, a poster appeared outside the Town Hall, saying: WANTED – a SALESMAN who has STOLEN the MAYOR'S CHAIN (and other objects). Underneath, was a photograph. It was an exact picture of the man who had gone off with the golden coin. But where was he now? The road mender went to see the mayor in person, and explained what had happened, and how he had seen the robber disappear down the crevice.

All sorts of people offered to descend to the bottom and bring him back – but although they fixed ropes and ladders and ventured down them, one after the other, they could find no one, and the bottom of the hole was as far away as ever. No one could reach it.

In the end, they had to give up and go home. The mayor ordered a new chain for himself, and vowed he would keep it under lock and key in future.

The dishonest salesman was never seen again. It's my opinion that the fairies got hold of him, and would not let him go. He would make a very useful servant for them, and could easily be whittled down to size. That is what happens to people who make unpleasant use of their gifts.

As for the road mender; he refused to fill in the crevice, in spite of a great many instructions to do so. And he would not give any reason why not.

'A secret is a secret – especially where magic is

concerned. One does not talk about such things,' he would answer. His wife promised never to exchange the old for the new again, without his permission.

And she never did.

Sometimes, though, when the road mender was rocking himself in his chair, and had a specially absent-minded look about him, she would pop round next door to chat to a neighbour.

'My husband prefers old things to new,' she would explain, putting sugar in her tea and stirring it. 'And dreams to common sense. Once, you know, he THOUGHT he saw a fairy. But I know better.'

Did she, though?

What do you think?